WHICH COLOUR IS IT?

WRITTEN BY MARIA L. LOPES

Which colour is it?

Text Copyright © 2013 **Maria L Lopes**

ISBN: 978-0-9926339-2-9

Credits:

green apple *by slafko*
bananas *by vierdrie*
purple flower *by babykrul*
flamingo *by exchu1952*
Teddy bear *by GiniMiniGi*
koala *by gselmes*
macaw *by papaleguas*
lightning *by csabavero*
window shutters *by mimbik*
sunflower *by duchessa*
waterdrop *by hummel 12*
easter egg *by greschoj*
camel *by ryas*

RED

Red watermelon sliced
and ready to eat.

GREEN

Green apple – fresh and tasty.

YELLOW

Yellow banana – yummy, yummy.

ORANGE

Orange juice good to drink.

PURPLE

Purple flowers are my favourite.

PINK
Pink Flamingo walking or dancing.
What a beautiful sight.

BLUE
Blue coat keeps me warm.
What a day!
I want to go out to play.

WHITE

White bib to keep me clean.
When I am eating.

BLACK
Black Bird singing in the warm sunlight.

BROWN

Brown soft bear and cuddling
comfortable to sleep.

GREY
Grey Koala is cute!

BLACK AND WHITE
Black and white penguins. Are they playing or is it a fight?

BLUE AND GOLD
Blue Gold Macaw it is very bright. Ka! Ka!

TURQUOISE
Turquoise window what a beautiful colour.

BRIGHT
YELLOW
Sunflowers are bright and yellow.

DUKE BLUE
Duke Blue lightning in the sky.

BRIGHT GREEN

Bright Green leaf is beautiful to the eye.

BLUE GREEN COLOUR
Blue Green, sweet to the taste.

CAMEL
COLOUR
Camel hump in the hot desert sand.

Some other books by Maria L. Lopes

A Good Scare
ISBN 978-1492129899 (sc)
ISBN 978-0-9926339-0-5 (e)

This is a message that has universal appeal, and presenting it with loveable animal characters makes the essence of the story accessible to even the youngest of children.

South American Rainforest Animals
ISBN 978-1-4684-7873-7 (sc)
ISBN 979-1-4684-7874-4 (e)

Brings readers up close with rainforest animals that are in danger of extinction of the loss habitat. Young children will enjoy exploring every page of this book.

Oliver the Sailor
When Oliver spent the day at the beach with his grandfather, he didn't expected an old sailing ship to take him on a wild adventure.

Available soon.

Terrific Trip!
A few months had passed since Tina the beluga whale had gone back home to the North Pole. Eddie and his friend Bella embaked in a wild adventure to reunite with they friend Tina. He didn't expected the holiday trip to take him on a terrific adventure.